The *Life Writing* **Work**book

How to Work through Your Life's Unresolved Emotional Experiences

Aihi

BALBOA.
PRESS
A DIVISION OF HAY HOUSE

Balboa Press books may be ordered through booksellers or by contacting:

Balboa Press
A Division of Hay House
1663 Liberty Drive
Bloomington, IN 47403
www.balboapress.com
1 (877) 407-4847

Because of the dynamic nature of the Internet, any web addresses or links contained in this book may have changed since publication and may no longer be valid. The views expressed in this work are solely those of the author and do not necessarily reflect the views of the publisher, and the publisher hereby disclaims any responsibility for them.

The author of this book does not dispense medical advice or prescribe the use of any technique as a form of treatment for physical, emotional, or medical problems without the advice of a physician, either directly or indirectly. The intent of the author is only to offer information of a general nature to help you in your quest for emotional and spiritual well-being. In the event you use any of the information in this book for yourself, which is your constitutional right, the author and the publisher assume no responsibility for your actions.

Any people depicted in stock imagery provided by Thinkstock are models, and such images are being used for illustrative purposes only.
Certain stock imagery © Thinkstock.

ISBN: 978-1-5043-3662-8 (sc)
ISBN: 978-1-5043-3663-5 (e)

Library of Congress Control Number: 2015911244

Print information available on the last page.

Balboa Press rev. date: 8/19/2015

Dedicated to human harmony

Testimonials

After having completed the writing series, the knot in the pit of my stomach, for the first time, is not there. I feel lightness, freedom, flexibility, openness and acceptance inside. And a much greater capacity to love myself and others. This has truly been an amazing experience. ~ Liala Y. ATL

It is so rare to be given permission to speak our truths and be respectfully heard. ~ Masani T. Ithaca

What I can offer without reservation is my appreciation for the work that you are doing and for how much of yourself you bring to your work with us. May the love that you so freely offer us come back to bless you many times over. Warmly, ~ Masani T. Ithaca

I am honored - through the process of life-writing - to connect more deeply to my essential nature and to recognize again, the rightness of my work as a psychiatrist. ~ Kristen N. Ithaca

This felt really different. I wrote out my stories with a beginning, middle, and end and found that monologuing to myself about my past and about who I was and what I was thinking was harder than I imagined. It felt different than participating in a dialogue with someone. It forced me to really look at myself and connect with what I was putting down on the page in a way I've never felt before with other forms of self expression and communication." ~Emma H. Cornell

This has brought me an interesting feeling of relief and gives my heart such tremendous satisfaction. I've noticed through my writing that the things I thought were affecting me, were not really important. Through my writing I found moments that had a huge impact on me and I had no idea the intensity of their worth. I compare life writing to cleaning out from underneath your bed. Things fall down there, things get tucked away, you may even intentionally hide things down there. Life Writing allows you to go through these things that are hidden down underneath and determine their worth to you. Things that are not meaningful-you throw out; pictures or memories that have sentimental value, you store neatly in their proper places. Once you've finished, you have decluttered your space and can breathe a sigh of relief. No more mess. No more baggage. ~ Daaiyah S. Atlanta

This is hard but everything tells me this is exactly where I need to be. ~ Michelle W. New York City

It's astounding how compelled I am to write between conference calls. ~ Siobhan M. Ithaca

I appreciated the peaceful, isolated time set aside to do this. I now have a lot better understanding of the <u>why</u> of so many things – especially in my immediate family and in regards to my boyfriend. I am also very calmed by this group and see the purpose of the community in this work. ~ Judith T. Cornell

"...in the face of some very undesirable conditions that will change someday, hopefully, strangely enough, I am not depressed for the first time in what seems like forever. It isn't that I am not sad.... It isn't that ever-present feeling though like it used to be. ~Daniel B. Cornell

The workshop series was deep and meaningful. For me, it brought to the surface the issues that I thought I had resolved, but now know still need work. The atmosphere was professional. The participants were so open and it was a space of safety and trust. I highly recommend this series to anyone seeking the gift of truth. Aihi led with professionalism, care and deep respect. ~Joan S. Ithaca

"I felt myself evolving through the life writing process." ~ Stephan M. Cornell

"I'm amazed. I've done a lot of work on myself already and I'm surprised at how this seems to tap important things. I'm fascinated by it. Wow." I find your work very complimentary to other course I'm taking and am deeply grateful for how it found me. We live in challenging times but, having said that I also see so much good going on—your workshop being one! ~ Siobhan M.

I loved the writing. I very much appreciate that you leave some thinking time for your questions to sink in. Tonight's writing has left me wanting to write more. I feel a door has been opened. .... I can see myself getting up tomorrow morning, hopping in the shower and getting on with my day. ~ Kim W. Ithaca

Thanks for your courage, humor and leadership. You rock! :-) ~Michelle W. NYC

This was very powerful. One of the exercises surprised me. It clarified a key thing I needed to have change. Thank you for the work you do! Aihi, I was very touched by tonight's session. I have been told several times in my life that I do not let people get to know me, that I am superficially friendly but then people hit a wall of my self-protectiveness. It was very moving for me to feel seen by people and that I allowed myself to be seen. Thank you for that gift. ~ Sharon S. Ithaca

I saw how attached I was when I called back a couple of times to the conference, eventually it kicked in to me that it was over. That must be tough work trying to figure out how to end such a powerful process. ~Natasha T. Ithaca College

Tonight's writing has left me wanting to write more. Thanks again...Kim W. Ithaca

The benefits of life writing are extensive, and life changing. Before life writing, I didn't really know who I was—I hadn't owned my story, my life, my past. I felt lost. The process of life writing has changed me. I know more about myself, I am confident that I can feel and own an emotion, and call it mine. I have met my life story, head on, and I have learned to live with and even love the parts I hadn't before. I've learned that being myself is the best person to be. And even more than all these things, even bigger than becoming more assertive, confident, and resilient...I have been taught to live life fully, completely, without inhibitions or worries about what other people might think. I have realized that who I am, and what I'm about, is something the world needs to see more of. The world is waiting for me, and I want to spend the rest of my life, giving my very best to the world. ~Justine L. Cornell

Life writing has helped me realize my goal of becoming a fully functioning happy and emotionalyy healthy adult. I took the course when I was 21. The course also gave me powerful tools for dealing with current difficult events productively. The skills and habits gained from Life Writing are helping me process complications in an extremely productive manner. Because of Life Writing, I am leaps and bounds ahead of the curve in my ability to deal with and learn from life's complications. I am not sure I would have ever had the courage to do that without Aihi's help and for that I am grateful. ~Daniel B. Cornell

"I found this to be incredibly useful. It differs so much from traditional methods which force you to face an issue abruptly and openly with someone you barely know. This allows you to touch upon issues only as far as you let it go, and there is no pressure to share since change is happening within by simply writing words on a page. I found myself more free, inspired, yet still full of emotion after the first session. My favorite part is that you don't have to leave with any action items other than letting your newly found feelings marinate over the course of the week. I am so excited to learn more about this process which I believe would be an innovative and effective way to reach out to individuals from different backgrounds and bridge the gaps defined by today's society." ~Katherine H.

And you, Aihi--just love you! :) I so appreciate you taking the time to see something wonderful in each of us. To let us know that we have potential, and possibilities, and that we are amazing people. Every time you listen to us, I feel heard, and every time you share with us, I feel strength. I have to say, this life writing is one of the best things that's happened to me. Thank you so much for this gift! Talk to you next week on the call. ~Justine L. Cornell

"I participated in Life Writing during my sophomore year in college. I did not know exactly what to expect from this program; I figured that Life Writing would just be one extended journal writing exercise, but it did so much more for me than basic journal writing could ever do. Life Writing really dug deep and helped me put what I want for my future into perspective. Aihi taught me a way through which to understand my past, come to terms with it, and move on. Life Writing is an invaluable tool that I will take with me from Cornell University and use for the rest of my life." ~ Ashemsa L. Cornell

"Marilou Awiakta, an Indigenous Cherokee author and former translator for the U.S. Air Force, has noted that "all people have poetry in them. Some can't write it, but the poet can listen intently to what people say and send it out into the world. It's a process of translation for the people." I love this quotation because it crystallizes what this has taught and done for me. Aihi too is a poet and a translator, giving voice and story to all of us, no matter how little poetry we think we have." ~ Irene L. Cornell

"...getting it out,...talking to you, but more talking to myself. Saying things I wouldn't normally say, but because of your questions, it's making me aware of myself..... I wouldn't even have started.... Things would have been still hanging, you see, in my background. And, like I said, it's only like until we did the thing on the paper...the mind map.... It gives you the reality. Plus we started out with the past. So there was a lot, a lot that was uncovered. So you have no idea, that maybe didn't get in the record...but it made me think...there was a lot of stuff that I never said. We never had enough time. There was a lot I had to think through. You started something in that class and I'm not going to stop until it's done. [I wish] more of the guys had come to the class. It could have touched everybody." ~Anonymous community research participant AT

During the 10 sessions, I came to appreciate the life writing process as a powerful tool for individual growth & development. And Aihi really knows her stuff! Her expert, gentle, and nonjudgmental guidance allows group members to learn and grow together. Thanks, Aihi! I have really enjoyed this process -- understanding life writing from the inside and experiencing you as you guide others in the life writing process --- so wonderful! ~ Risa B. New Jersey

"It was real helpful...in changing, even back in my childhood days, some things I had to cope with. I was able to forgive...and... put the past behind and... look toward the future. Everything is out of the way. I just have to go about getting everything in process by doing things. ~Anonymous community research participant ATL

"This helped clear the clutter from my mind, heart, and soul, leaving a safe space for creativity, love, and growth. People for whom I previously had little respect, I now understand better and am more able to forgive. ~ Christa D. Cornell

"[The workshops] helped me to speak out more. You have to let a person know where you are, if not they will just keep on doing what they want to do and you will still be in the same little bind, scared to speak out. ...When we started talking about our childlife and how we went on about that....By just sitting down expressing, discussing about each person's... stuff. It helped me a lot because it released me." ~Anonymous community research participant ATL

"I knew this would provoke a consciousness of unresolved issues, but I did not comprehend the degree that this would help me process and purge those issues." ~ Willie S. New Jersey

"When I heard you speak, I knew this is what I need. I'm excited about your workshops. It's like once you get some of the old garbage out, digging in talking about your past and stuff, it gives you a more solid foundation to go on. The best thing about it for me was when we did the sessions sharing about our visions.... You know,... [that] was a big, big thing for me." ~Anonymous community research participant ATL

"This is very powerful, because when it's just you and the paper, there are no defenses from the truth, as felt by your heart. Aihi creates an involved, deeply personal space where people can experience unresolved issues and channel those emotions into building a personal, lasting, and coherent sense of purpose. Given the experiences and insight that we're gaining from this, me and a group of others doing this work would like to expand it to the general youth of the community. We believe that a community outreach program of this nature would help youth (especially those at-risk of making destructive decisions as a function of their experiences) to cope, and construct and apply a meaningful sense of purpose and direction to their lives." ~Joanna S. Cornell

"I would recommend this type of work to everyone I know. Aihi has an incredible talent for helping others analyze and clarify their life experiences and memories as well as helping others find the meaning of them. She cares deeply about all of the individuals she presents this rewarding experience to and she improved my quality of life." ~Paola T. Cornell

Dear Aihi,

I am so happy to have been a part of your life story. Thank you for introducing me to life writing which has changed the way I view my life and how I interact with those around me. This will forever be a part of who I am. I am so grateful! All the best, ~ Kathy H. Cornell

"I know you're probably tired of hearing me say this. Aihi was a very very important part of my life, because there was no one to listen to me. I had people around me, my family, but, you know, I guess they say, "Get over it girlfriend. You'll be alright." I was about to have a nervous breakdown. Really, I believe I think I already had one, but didn't realize it. I was just barely functioning. The workshops made the difference in my life – the communication, the talking. I was able to sit down and express myself. It took a while because I'm not the type of person... use to be the type of person that didn't open up, but now I do. I don't know how to express it. I don't know the words for it. It was Aihi. The way she was always there and always made herself down to earth. She always started out with the way things worked out for herself and the way things happened to her. It was like she wasn't sitting interviewing, sitting there pure. I don't know how to put it into words. I walked around for a long time with something on my heart that I wouldn't tell anybody, and I was able to let other people know about it and that was liberating. I just needed someone to reach out to me." ~ Anonymous community research participant ATL

"I was able to dig deep within myself and think about the people closest to me."
~ Anonymous student evaluation Cornell

Life Writing has helped me find myself in ways that I would have never thought. Initially going into this project, I didn't really think I needed it or that it would really have any affect on me. I usually write when I have something bothering me, and I already was confident in who I am and knew what I wanted in life. I was also mentally stable and didn't have many fears in my life that I was avoiding. Because of all these things, I felt that the Life Writing Project would just be something nice to do, but not particularly beneficial to me. These initial thoughts changed as weeks progressed and meetings became more intense. This project really allowed me to understand myself better, learning why I do some of the things I do and why I have some of the relationships that I have. It helped me to think back on events of my childhood and finally put closure to them. This project was refreshing, self-building, and healthy. And everyone, no matter where they are in life, should experience this." ~ Marian S. Cornell

"I appreciated having focused time set aside each week to think and write about the important relationships in my life. Life writing gave me a chance to start to clarify what I would like to do next in my life and to see what type of obstacles I tend to put in my own path." ~ Jen M. Cornell

"There's some healin' goin' on!" ~ Ira R. Ithaca

I wish to let you know how greatly your work and studies have affected my life. I've been meaning to put down in words how grateful I am for the work we did in the lifewriting sessions. Looking back on the past two years since I completed the lifewriting workshops, many great things have happened in my life. It was just recently that I made the connection between the great and mighty changes in my life to the reflections and concentrated efforts of writing through my life's experiences. Aihi, you are truly an inspiration to me. I trust you with my heart and my feelings. I tore out a few pages from my journal that I want to share with you as feedback and an update expressing how lifewriting has helped me to grow and move forward in my life. Thank you for following your dreams and for helping me to realize mine. Daaiyah S. ATL

Contents

Chapter One

Introduction

In this chapter, I will introduce a workshop series called Life Writing. Life Writing is eight sessions of deeply engaging private writing through your life story in a specialized manner. It focuses primarily on working through a certain set of unresolved life experiences, certain difficult experiences that have gone unacknowledged and unexamined. I stumbled upon Life Writing at age twenty-nine. I was at that moment in a divorce when you know it's over and it's time to move on. I realized how little I understood my life, and that I had no real sense of how to make a life. I wanted a life. I wanted a certain kind of satisfaction with life that I knew existed. Yet, here I was, very clear that this marriage wasn't going to work out and faced with raising a lovely child alone, as I made my way toward this certain something I couldn't even name.

I moved in with my best friend's parents, who were very kind to me. To try to get a handle on things, I secluded myself in their basement for many evenings to dissect my life story. It was just instinct. Starting with my earliest memory, I started the walk forward, sifting carefully through each experience I could recall. I noticed that some of my memories required more time and attention than others. I would approach certain memories in the writing and my body would tighten. At first, I just kept going. But those particular memories called me back to them. So I went back, slowed down, and sifted more carefully, -- looking at the scene, the circumstances, the people involved, and at myself and my emotions, my perceptions, my fears.

The tightness in my body became my clue for where to look the closest. I learned to back up and write through those memories again and sometimes even again. At one point, I labeled this part of the process 'wet-writing'. I cried so many tears.

At the end of this rather intense process, I felt light and free and clear. I can't tell you how long it took, but it was weeks, a couple months perhaps.... There was no doubt that something in me had shifted. I felt a new sense of self-possession. I felt very present in my own body and aware of myself in a way I wasn't before. I can see this same new presence arise in the faces of others as they complete the Life Writing process.

This shift has been my obsession now for more than 25 years. Studying it has led me through two master's degrees, a Ph.D., and to my career as a narrative psychologist and university professor. This series of Life Writing workshops will walk you through your own process of Life Writing following the same steps I took. To give you more of a sense of what you might expect after Life Writing, let me tell you the stories of a couple more Life Writers. These are not their real names, of course.

Delores is an African American woman who was in her mid-thirties when we met. In many ways, she had a middle class upbringing. Until her father died, she grew up with both parents. Both of them worked, so there were two incomes supporting the household.

Her family didn't move around a lot, but lived in a single-family home, and in the same house and neighborhood her entire childhood. She attended the same schools and had the same friends. What she needed, materially, her parents were able to and did provide. However, Delores's mother ridiculed her quite severely. Delores's sister was her mother's favorite. Delores said her mother never made her feel special in any way. She also said she looked just like her mother.

Her father was away a lot as a cab driver, and he was also mean when he was home. She spoke of how very much she loved him despite this, as we all do, and of how they tried to convince him to stay home the day he died in a car crash.

So, while Delores's parents were physically present, neither of them was emotionally warm toward her. Delores had never stopped to think about how this might have affected her. When I met Delores, she had four gorgeous children born from a loving long-term relationship with her partner. She had bought a house. She was a school bus driver and she loved driving. She loved her job and had earned attendance awards at work.

She really wanted to move up in the company. She said that if she just had a little more education, she could do it and gave the sense that that one barrier loomed large between her and a higher position. She had made no efforts to obtain a higher position.

One year after Life Writing, we talked again, and she tells me she now has the supervisor position and is looking to move up in the company again. I asked her how that happened. Here is roughly what she said.

> I got my resume and cover letters together, and I handed copies to everyone in the meeting. I presented myself professionally to them and I let them know I really wanted the position. I simply told them that I was not going to train another person for a job that I wanted and could do well. I told them I wanted the position, and they gave me the position.

Note that the language used prior to Life Writing centered on her personal shortcomings and the barriers between her and what she wanted, "If I had just a little bit more education…," while the language used after Life Writing conveyed her personal effectiveness, "I simply told them that I was not going to train another person for a job that I wanted and could do well." She was unambivalent about her intention, and her own certainty was trusted by those who hired her. Delores also told me of other areas in her life where she demonstrated this new level of personal effectiveness and self-possession.

Walter was about the same age as Delores, maybe a little older. He was a recovering alcoholic. He was working at a furniture store and attending church regularly. Just a basically cheerful and kind sort of guy. Always smiling.

After Life Writing, Walter noticed that the people who bought the furniture he sold often had no way to get the furniture home. So he purchased a truck and started delivering the furniture after hours. After some time, he decided he wanted to purchase a house. He had some unpaid debts to track down. He tracked those down, paid them off, and after a little time purchased the house. I can't recall when he first indicated that he needed to reconnect with his daughter. However, when I spoke with him in recent months, I learned that he did reconnect with her and remains an integral part of his daughter's life.

The furniture Walter's customers bought needed delivering before he completed the workshop series. However, only afterwards did he take notice of it and actually do something about it. The same is true in regards to the house and his relationship with his daughter. Delores, Walter, and I were able to make what is recognized as a pivotal shift in human psycho-emotional growth and development. Abraham Maslow labeled this a shift from deficiency to being - from fearing that something that we can't quite put our finger on is missing or that we are lacking in some unidentifiable way, to relaxing into a sense of completeness and capability.

Over time, this shift leads to much more than personal effectiveness, but this sense of personal effectiveness and all that follows it is routinely obstructed by unresolved emotional experiences. This is where Life Writing is useful.

As I stated earlier, Life Writing is eight sessions of deeply engaging private writing through your life story in a specialized manner. It is *private* writing so that you can be deeply honest with yourself on the page without concern for whether someone else will ever see or read what you write. You don't have to be concerned about spelling or grammar. The idea is simply for you to write honestly and deeply about certain life experiences.

Starting now and throughout these chapters, I will teach you how to Life Write, but first, here is a brief overview of the series. In this first chapter, you will be introduced to the concept of Life Writing and the Life Writing process. In chapters two-four, you will practice what Clifford Geertz called "thick" description of minor but meaningful life events; and practice connecting with your interior emotional experience. Think for a moment about what I might mean by the term, "thick" description. The first idea that comes to mind, of course, is thick versus thin, and you are right. In practicing thick description, you practice capturing the relevant details of your memories – the details that matter. You also practice finding the words that best represent your feelings and interpretations of experiences at the time they occurred. You practice including as much detail as possible of each moment in an important experience. You learn to take your time and to sift carefully through the layers to understand precisely what your important experiences have meant for you. This will require slow presence in certain moments of your life and careful tuning-in to the quality of what was going on. Don't worry, I will guide you step-by-step.

When I say *minor* but meaningful life events, this is to say that Life Writing begins with experiences that carry light meaning, but meaning nonetheless, then slowly increases the depth and intensity of memory-examination. Life Writing focuses on a certain set of experiences that are common to all humans (though they vary by culture), although few of us slow down long enough to go inward and look around at our life the way Life Writing guides you to do. Nothing we cover in this series is unimportant.

In chapters five-eight, you will write privately about *deeply* meaningful life events including your earliest experiences in your family and community; your early experiences of love and affection or the lack of love and affection experienced in your early years; and about traumatic moments you can recall. In the ninth chapter, you will turn from all this and complete exercises designed to lead you toward your own inner guidance. Exercises that are designed to re-align you with that which you find most important and that which only you can know gives your life its meaning. In the final chapter, we discuss where to go from here.

Now let me give you a little more detail about the writing sessions so you can make an informed decision about whether or not you want to proceed through the Life Writing process at this time. Some people decide they are not ready to do their narrative work, and that is a perfectly appropriate decision in some cases. I fully respect that choice and only want to guide you through Life Writing when you are ready. Life Writing is hugely rewarding, but the middle four sessions involve intense emotional work.

You're in the first session - the Introduction to Life Writing. In sessions two and three, you will practice thick description, as mentioned earlier, as well as begin to get in touch with your inner emotional experience. Session four is titled 'Your Childhood Home' and continues with more of the same, but also begins to get a little more personal. By this time, you will want to reference the emotions list provided by changingminds.org (see the 'short tree structure' (http://changing-minds.org/explanations/emotions/basic%two0emotions.htm) for help in identifying your precise emotions. Identifying your precise emotions is a *very* important aspect of Life Writing. I will say much more about this as we go along.

Beginning at session five, you begin to earn the shift that Life Writing promises when done properly. In session five, I will spend a good bit of time setting the stage for your writings through sessions five, six, and seven. In session five, your *interpretations* of your experiences with your Mother are the central focus. Note that I emphasize the phrase 'your interpretations', for this is what matters in Life Writing. It may seem at first, that this session is about your mother. It isn't. It is about you and how you interpreted your experiences with her. Your interpretation of events - the meaning you gave to them at the time - is what we sift out from the pages of your life story throughout this process.

Here are some of the actual questions so you get a fuller sense of this critically important session.

> "If you do not know the answer to some of the questions, write what it feels like not to know. You may also answer this list of questions for another significant mother-figure(s) in your life, however do not omit writing about an absent biological mother or a mother you never knew."

> "What three words best describe the person who became your mother?"

> "What were some of her dreams?"

> "What did she do when she was at home?"

"Did she seem to understand you or have a sense of what you needed or wanted? In other words, did she get you?"

Session six is exactly like session five, except it is about your interpretations of your experiences with your father. I've had people say, he wasn't there, I never knew him, I have nothing to write. However, there are always many emotions around his having been absent that will need to be written through. I have yet to meet anyone who never knew their father or mother who had not held on to any scrap of information about him or her that had ever come across their radar. There seems always work to be done here.

Session seven is about the traumatic events in your life that you know you will never forget; those traumatic experiences that changed you forever. These might have occurred in any area of your life. Session eight allows you the time to finish out any leftovers from sessions five, six, and seven, and guides your return to an exercise begun in session seven around significant traumas. Session nine guides you through some exercises that help you to recognize and align with the part of your inner guidance that you can trust the most. The concept of *prepotency* in human development theory suggests that there is a part of your inner guidance that knows how to unfold once certain unresolved experiences are addressed. You will look for instances in your life story when your inner guidance seemed most apparent and grapple with what those instances might mean or suggest for future direction. In the final session, session ten, I will suggest possible next steps.

You may wonder why you are asked to write through these memories versus talk through them. There *is* a talking part of the Life Writing process, which I will explain in chapter ten, but I've used the analogy of a treadmill vs a conveyor belt when explaining the difference between talking and writing through an un-resolved emotional experience.

A treadmill goes round and round, while a conveyor belt moves its contents farther and farther away. Talking through these experiences is quite powerful, but seems to leave them in place to return again and again for more process-ing it seems, while writing out these experiences seems to do something differ-ent with them.

First, writing slows down the process of working through the memory, and gives you more time to extract more information and more understanding from them as you go along. Second, writing memories of experiences down seems to give them a place outside yourself. On the conveyor belt, over time, they move farther and farther away and less and less relevant to your day to day existence and to your capacity to do whatever you are doing. There is more to be said about this.

I want to reiterate that a key element of Life Writing is accurately identifying and precisely labeling emotions. The emotions list at changingminds.org (short tree structure) helps you to distinguish the finer differences between emotions.

You must pay close attention to what you feel at any given moment as you write through your story. Again, don't you worry, I will walk you through how to listen and attend to yourself and to sense what you feel and to know what to write.

I tell you and trust you with the details of my own story throughout the Life Writing process. I do this to model for you the vulnerability you are to risk, as well as the resilience or new strength you can expect if you do so sufficiently. For me, this is a sacred offering of myself, and I only do this in the context of helping others get their narrative work done. In all my years of doing this work, Life Writers have embraced this offering of myself with respect and courtesy and have used my story to power their own honesty with themselves about their own pain, so they, too, can shift into gear. Mind you that the parts of my story that I tell here have been fine-tuned and shortened quite a bit for the purposes of this workbook. The first writing of my story was nowhere near as poetic as it has become over these many years. The first writing of your own story will be much longer as you grapple slowly, deeply, and honestly with the many elements of it.

Research shows that most people can effectively do this kind of guided life review on their own. I was alone in a basement when I did my own Life Writing, and while I felt emotions more deeply than I ever had before, the process was perfectly safe for me. If done properly, you will experience some temporary sadness when remembering difficult experiences. However, in my 20+ years of guiding this particular uncovering process, I have known only one person to require additional psychological assistance and a couple people who have sought additional counseling to help them remember more of their life stories. Experts in this field recognize that this kind of revisiting life experiences is normal human behavior with little to no risk other than temporary sadness. Still, I have always required those I work with in person to identify at least one mental health professional they can consult should the need for additional support arise while completing this Life Writing process. I encourage you to do the same. Although the need for additional help is unlikely, I'd rather we err on the side of caution. You might check with your county for a guide to local mental health services if you do not already know how to identify a mental health professional. The temporary sadness you are likely to feel is the price we pay for the wide range of mental, physical, and social health benefits many people experience after Life Writing. Also, as you know, you are free to skip any questions you do not want to write about or to quit the Life Writing process altogether at any time.

My work is designed for non-depressed persons going about their everyday lives. It is also suitable for persons with mild or moderate depression. It is not designed or suitable for persons with severe psychological challenges. If you are currently under severe distress or experiencing severe psychological challenges, do not proceed to Life Write on your own. Seek the help of a trained mental health professional. Expressive writing, which is what Life Writing is, has a long history of generating well-being among non-depressed and mild to moderately depressed persons. It has been facilitated by professionals and non-professionals as well as self-administered or done on one's own. I have worked effectively with young, middle-aged, and older adults, and with men and women of many different races and ethnic backgrounds. Still, I must include here the following disclaimer:

> Please note, that your choice to proceed with this Life Writing process signifies your agreement to accept full responsibility in the unlikely event of harm arising out of or in connection with these guided Life Writing sessions. This liability release extends to and covers all known and unknown or unforeseen injuries, damages, or losses.

Now, here are some guidelines to prepare yourself for the Life Writing process, which begins in the next chapter. Take yourself away from the busy-ness of your life for the time that you write. Find a time and place of silence, then make your body as comfortable as possible – wear lose, warm clothes, for example. You will need a pen or pencil for writing. Allow about two hours for each writing session. You might not use all the time, but you don't want to feel at all rushed. Allow some space between the writing sessions, a week in between is good. This will give you ample time to recall and process thoroughly within each session. Drop any idea of anyone in any part of your story, including yourself, as being good or bad or right or wrong. That will only distract you from the goal, which is simply to finally understand *your* truth and *your* life. Just sift carefully through your memories, examine them, listen for what only they can tell you about your life. The memories inside you are not dead, but very much alive and impacting you in every moment you live.

Commit to the struggle of communicating. Keep trying until what is inside you is accurately transferred to the page. If you know you're close to the truth of an experience but still feel there is more, go over it again and write in the missing pieces.

Finally, take the person you were at the time of any particular experience seriously – assume that what she or he wants to say to you about the experience is what is important and not what you might say now about the experience in retrospect or looking back at it. Again, don't worry, I will walk you through this process and remind you of these guidelines as we go along.

Think of this as a sacred time that you take for yourself and a sacred undertaking, for it very much is on so many levels. Give yourself a couple hours in a quiet, undisturbed place to do the writing exercises. Quiet your outer world long enough to actually get your narrative work done once and for all.

So welcome to Life Writing. I'm so very excited to join with you in this growth experience. Thank you for choosing to do your narrative work, and I look forward to beginning the writing process with you in chapter two.

Chapter Two

What's In a Name?

In this chapter, you will begin the process of actually writing through your life story. Remember, Life Writing is a structured process, so please do not proceed if you have not read carefully through chapter one, the introduction and understand both the benefits and risks of Life Writing. This writing session is called 'What's In a Name?' Before we get into the writing exercise for today, I want to say more about how to Life Write. It is important that I teach you how to do this as we go along.

In Life Writing, you don't *think* your way to your truth, you *feel* your way to the truth. You feel what is to go onto the page, then you use your thinking to write what you feel. Your truth will be found in what you *feel*. Most of us in the west have been trained thoroughly in thinking our way through life. The thinking part of us is well-developed, so you will likely have to adjust to this idea of feeling your way through this Life Writing process. Life Writing seeks a certain truth that can only be found in your emotions – what you have *felt*. What you have felt, is then made sense of by both your emotions *and* your mind. So, the truth that is to be written onto your page will be discovered by a close and accurate examination of your feelings related to the events and experiences you will be guided to write through. You are likely to develop a certain emotional wisdom as a result of these eight writing sessions that can serve you long into the future. You are to attend to the *precise* emotions in your body at the time of writing, which, if done properly, will mirror what you felt at the time the event occurred. Just take this in for now.

Another related item is that complete accuracy of memory is not exactly what we are after. What we are after is your interpretation of events at the time of their occurrence. I alluded to this in chapter one, but it bears repeating again and again. The focus is on the *interpretations* you made of events at the time of their occurrence. These writing tips become more and more relevant as we move through the process.

TODAY'S WRITING ASSIGNMENT

The writing exercise for today is about your First Name. Make sure you have a quiet, undisturbed couple hours for writing. You likely won't need the entire two hours today, but you will in most of the future sessions. Please write out your answers to the following questions:

How did you get your first name? In other words: Who named you? Is there a story around receiving that name?

What is the meaning of your name? This is easily looked up online, if you don't already know. Sources don't always agree. I say pick the meaning that resonates the most!

Do you like your name?

What name would you choose for yourself if you were choosing?

What nicknames have you been given over the years?

Who gave you those nicknames, and what were their motives?

MY NAME STORY

My chosen name is Aihi which stands for the phrase, 'All instants are holy instants'. I've had many nicknames. My favorite by far is the way my mom would almost sing it, Aihiiiii? My uncle Rob, who came to visit us each Christmas, called me Skinny Minny. He was a big, round, happy-faced man whose eyes rested on us with such love. They just glistened when he looked at us. He loved my Dad - who really needed that - and all his eleven children. He would fill his station wagon with oranges, grapefruit, and nuts every year at Christmas time. His great big belly would shake when he laughed, and through those warm and glistening eyes he would look at me and say, 'OOOH Skinny Minny.' Heh, heh, heh.'

My dad called me Skinny-legs-and-all. Perhaps you're getting a picture of what I looked like in those days. And then there was this girl in high school who made fun of my buck teeth. I eventually got braces after I grew up and starting earning my own money, but her nickname for me wasn't in words - just her gesture of fingers hanging out of the front of her mouth when she walked passed me. It's Ok if you're laughing. I'm laughing now, too, but it wasn't funny at the time.

That's it for me. Now it's your turn. Writing your answers to these questions will start to give you practice in attending to yourself. If you finish this session and have time left over, feel free to move on to chapter three. This is the only time when it is OK to work through more than one session in one sitting as this one can be relatively brief for some people. Don't rush it, though. Enjoy the pleasure of beginning to write your story in a slow, contemplative fashion. There are some overflow pages at the end of the journal – you might need those for some of the writing sessions. Thank you, again, for choosing to do your narrative work, and I look forward to continuing the Life Writing process with you in chapter three.

<u>Your writing: What's In a Name?</u>

_____

_____

_____

_____

_____

_____

_____

_____

_____

_____

_____

_____

_____

_____

_____

_____

_____

Chapter Three

Your Story of Best Friendship

This writing session is titled, 'Your Story of Best Friendship'. In this session you're going to practice 'thick description', which means you will practice finding words that capture the subtle meanings in your life experiences. You will also practice getting in touch with your inner emotional experience. But first, a lot more on how to Life Write.

When Life Writing, you have to think small. Write about one small self-contained incident that is still vivid in your memory. Pause in moments. Stay with a word, a reaction, an inaction. Don't hurry past, but stay until you have teased out all it's contents. In today's writing you are asked to be in a particular moment, then transfer that moment to the page.

You are also to think few. We are looking for the critical few highly impactful experiences in your lifetime. Some experiences may have occurred repeatedly, over and over again in one of your important relationships. All experiences of a similar type in a relationship can be managed all at once by selecting the one that epitomizes or best reflects the dynamic of it and writing thoroughly through just that one. I'll say more about this later. Once we identify these critical few highly impactful life experiences, we are going to unpack them. The stronger the emotions in your body, the more important is the memory for unpacking. Hesitance also suggests importance. These are the ones we will unpack.

You are to think episodes. Like your favorite TV show – beginning, middle, and end. Ever seen a movie that in the end only covered a few minutes of actual reality? We're going to slow everything down and take an entire movie size view of a single experience. Only by expanding it this way can we get out of it what is there to be learned. When you are finished writing your story, your narrative should be mostly little stories. You will write your first one today. It is absolutely incredible how much more a story can teach us versus a report. I will teach you how to write your significant experiences as the stories they are. As you do this, you will be in the experiences again as you write them, and you will have access, again, to the exact emotions you are to inscribe onto the page. These stories can teach you so much about yourself. Plan to be surprised.

You are to capture the details. Being in your experiences again, so to speak, as you write them, is how you get the details. It's not as difficult as it may seem. You may find that you are not satisfied that the experience and its meaning are clearly reflected there on the page. It is very likely that you will have to return to the narrative a few times until you feel that certainty that your truth has been identified and placed on the page. This is the work of Life Writing. If you do Life Writing well once, it is done forever for the experiences you unpacked.

Don't look for order or tidy connections in your story. Your emotions will tell you which way to go. Just trust those emotions. Be ready to be surprised by what was of true significance to you.

Finally, for today, show don't tell. Write so that if someone else were reading what you wrote they too would see what happened. Just show the experience, and let the fictitious reader interpret it. You may find that the first time you attempt to write an experience as a story, you simply report what happened. Even after I demonstrate how to 'show' it, you are likely to revert back to your normal way of telling or describing your experiences. Life Writing is a skill that requires a little practice, and this is the purpose of the present writing session - to give you a chance to practice.

Here is an example of show don't tell.

> I am in the spacious den of a warm, affluent, married couple – a tall, dark, healthy African man of about 70 or so years and his same-age wife, an elegant and sophisticated European woman. They are equals. I am at their home and they are relaxing – dressed in comfortable lounging clothes. We are new to each other, but we know each other somehow as we move easily about the space. Prosperity is apparent everywhere. I am in their home with free access and a sense of their complete and open generosity toward me. Then we are in a car and hungry. I have some unshucked corn

on the cob. We all have some. I have a few ears left - put back and away, because I have no idea where I will get my next meal. The wife asks for more. I look through what I have, three ears, I believe, and select the best for her, which in the end are the last two ears, because one is no good and the remaining two still have a few good kernels on them, the rest not properly formed. Living in the moment, I let the last two ears of corn go to where they are needed now. Then I notice the older man paying attention to this, and that it was a test to see whether I would share my last. The woman is enjoying the corn, as the man's hand comes to rest on my right knee. His touch is relaxed and loving - resting completely there as if we are one. We are being chauffeured. I am sitting between them, feeling flanked by them. She is sitting to my left and he is sitting to my right. She is wearing a cream colored dress made of a lined, sheer, flowing fabric that falls in soft layers comfortably toward her body. She rests comfortably in the seat with her legs together and touching mine. She is subtly and beautifully jeweled, unpretentious. I feel these are the most genuine people, as rich to the core in their shared level of human development as in their material life. Spirits-in-bodies. Glowing. Everything about them is elegant. He is wearing the finest black suit – the rich black wool lays against him begging to be touched – a gleaming white shirt and a narrow black tie. He is a strong, healthy, comfortably elegant, uninhibited, warm older man – an absolute match to his wife, clearly of many years. They are a couple, easy with each other, unhurried. We are all sitting comfortably close together in the back seat of this car, as if we are deeply connected friends. They are larger than I am, but not so much. I never quite see the white woman's face, but his is dark and smooth and just a little largish. I watch his mouth move as he talks with his wife, responding to something she must have said or asked. My face is right next to his, and I just let my eyes take him in, the pink lining of his dark lips as they move, his glistening teeth, his clear white eyes, the absolute health in his face. I let my eyes rest on him, taking him in.

Now take a moment to write down your interpretation of the dream. Just write a brief interpretation here:

_____

_____

_____

_____

_____

_____

_____

Now look at your interpretation of the experience I showed you earlier, it was a dream, actually, and ask yourself whether I told you that. I merely showed an experience and you saw in it whatever you did. Stories are extremely efficient tools for this work, so in this exercise, I need you to show me an experience. Here is how you <u>tell</u> me what happened when you went to the grocery store for bread:

> I went to the store for bread and the shelves were completely empty.
> I forgot it was Easter Sunday.

Here is how you <u>show</u> me what happened when you went to the grocery store for bread:

> My eyes were still half closed as I made my way down the bread isle. Without even thinking, I reached for the baguettes but my fingers landed on a cold metal shelf. Then I heard the church bells. Easter decorations hung from the ceiling.

TODAY'S WRITING ASSIGNMENT

Your writing task for today is to show best friendship. Show the moment when you knew you could truly trust this person. Show the episode, the experience, what happened, so that a fictitious reader can also know you could trust this person. Leave the fictitious reader nodding in recognition of deep trust and best friendship.

MY STORY OF BEST FRIENDSHIP

I have a best friend I have trusted for almost 30 years. It's a typical Sunday afternoon in the boarding house I shared with about eight other college students. My room door is open when the front door opens wide and this girl walks, or I should say glides through the front door, across the front room and kitchen, and into the room toward the back of the house. She was trailed by a tall, slender guy, probably her brother, and what appeared to be her easy feeling parents.

She wore all black with a bright, colorful scarf streaming from her neck. I took notice. Was she a dancer? The next time I saw her she was in the kitchen like she owned it cooking something that looked different than anything I knew of, so I asked her what it was. "It's tofu," she said. "Wanna taste?" I moved right into her generosity and openness and felt very much at home learning about vegetarianism and admiring her short afro. We found ourselves together a lot after that, just seemed natural. She had a boyfriend who we will call Deryk. Deryk had a friend named Andy. The four of us found deep resonance together and spent lots of time doing such a variety of things – cooking, games, restaurants, movies, bookstores, book-discussions, parties…. Lots and lots of laughter. One day, seems like another Sunday to me, based on what I recall myself doing, I'm in my room and unexpectedly, Vanessa is suddenly in my room and in tears. "What's wrong?!" I ask. She is a little hesitant, but clearly needs to tell me something. "I, I, I, think Deryk likes you!'" she says and catches her breath. The look of vulnerability and anticipation in her face leaves me not feeling accused, but trusted with her heart. I take her shoulders, and look squarely into her eyes. In very measured words, I say something like, "In all my interactions with Deryk, he has never so much as hinted at such a thing in any shape or form. I have no sense of any truth to that idea." We embraced, cried a little, and let that energy pass from us.

Your turn. Show the moment you knew you could trust your best friend. If you've never had a best friend, write what it's like not to have one and what a best friendship would look and feel like to you. If you have many 'best' friends, select one of them and show the moment. Once again, thank you for choosing to do your narrative work. I look forward to continuing the Life Writing process with you in chapter four.

Your Story of Best Friendship:

_____

_____

_____

_____

_____

_____

_____

_____

_____

_____

_____

_____

_____

_____

_____

_____

_____

_____

_____

Chapter Four

Your Childhood Home

This writing session is titled, 'Your Childhood Home". In this session you will continue to practice thick description and to show rather than tell experiences. You will also begin to move cautiously toward what may have been difficult spaces. Not everyone's childhood home was a difficult space, but many were - at least in some ways.

In terms of Life Writing, you will need to retain what is called 'unity of point of view'. What this means is that you are to retrieve the perspective you had at the age you were at the time of the events you write about, and you are *to retain that perspective* throughout the writing of that experience. The younger-you is the person who must narrate the text, this is the person speaking, not you at the age you are now. You are to write the words, thoughts, feelings, and interpretations of the younger-you, not the current you. Let her or him speak. She or he has needed to speak for a long time. Stop for a moment to think about this.

Think about the words you have just read. The trick to *successful* Life Writing is this – to allow the younger-you to express the emotions she or he felt at that time. He or she will access those emotions as s/he shows you the experience. The challenge is to recapture your perspective at the time of the event without clouding it with any present or more mature interpretations.

When experiences were really difficult, it is helpful to recall that the experience has already happened. It is now only a memory, although it can feel very real again. We tend to remember childhood experiences with the child's heart, and so you might hesitate to go there. It's OK, you are not that child anymore, *and I hope you are somewhere safe and secure.*

You will need to mentally place yourself again in the earlier moments, to re-experience the surroundings, the feelings, the observations and the interactions. To be the child you were. To let the persons discussed be the persons they were then, not who they might be now. To let the events happen again. You must recapture the quality and texture of the moment, and out of respect for the person you were then in whatever circumstances, some mourning may be necessary. Robin Sharma wrote that, "Change is hard at first, messy in the middle, and gorgeous at the end."

From here on, you are looking for the right emotion and the right word to identify it. In the moment when you find the right emotion, in that moment you will find yourself. Continually identify the precise emotions generated by your experiences. Let these travel through your hand and onto the page.

TODAY'S WRITING ASSIGNMENT

For today, you are to find an experience that captures what it was like for you to be in your childhood home or one that shows what was most important to you about your childhood home. If you find this difficult to recall, you might begin by showing the room in your childhood home that holds the most significance for you. What was most important to you is always completely idiosyncratic. For example, one person began by showing the wall-paper, because everything in her room was always Disney – the wall paper, the bedspread, the clothes, the picture frames.... Perhaps you felt homeless going to one parent's house during the week and the other on the weekend. Select and show an experience that captures this. Perhaps you were homeless in the real sense. Select and show an experience that captures this. Perhaps you moved a lot. Select an experience that shows how this made you feel. You might select the place that comes to mind when you say the word, "home" and write a story showing what was most important about that place. Perhaps your parents died or for some other reason were not present and you lived with another family member....

THE STORY OF MY CHILDHOOD HOME

My story has been worked on for quite some time and has become somewhat poetic, but don't let that obscure the real shame I felt as a girl and early teenager. On one occasion I led a boy to my neighbor's house when he walked me home, because I didn't want him to see where I lived. Here's this part of my story as I have come to show it. It includes a brief glimpse of my father.

My father worked at a local drug store. He laced and tied his polished black shoes before going out on Friday and Saturday nights. Before leaving the house he would flash us the friendliest grin, run his hand across his slick black hair and say, "Good stuff chile." We would all grin back eagerly, hoping to hold him that way for a while; reminded as he continued out the door that his pleasure had little to do with us. We all listened for the faintest sounds of his car as he drove away. Then we relaxed, grateful at least for an evening free of the whimsical wrath of Daddy.

We lived for years in a weather-beaten, four-room house that was coming apart at the seams. It had a pointed, rusting tin roof. All toilets, running water, and means for heating and air were outside. There were thirteen of us including my parents, and we were one of the poorest families in the small western town.

I believe this begins to give you a sense of why I needed to write through my family home experience in my efforts to understand what had influenced my sense of myself. In today's writing assignment, go toward any stories that capture something difficult about your childhood home in as much detail as possible. The good or positive memories are not the ones that imprison us or prevent free access to our creativity and usefulness to the world. It is the difficult or negative memories that do this. Take your time and bring a moment from your childhood home to life again for the period of this writing. Once again, thank you for choosing to do your narrative work. I look forward to continuing the Life Writing process with you in chapter five.

Your Childhood Home

_____

_____

_____

_____

_____

_____

_____

_____

_____

_____

_____

_____

_____

_____

_____

_____

Chapter Five

You and Your Mother

The title of this writing session is 'You and your mother', with the emphasis on you and not on your mother. In this session you will write through some of your experiences with your mother, focusing on your most intimate interpretations of those experiences and how they made you feel. The idea is not to imagine or assume that you have understood your mother's intentions. The idea is simply to learn and clarify what the younger-you was feeling and thinking. It is important to retain this focus and not fall into delineating what you perceive as her shortcomings. I know of no culture where elders are not held in high esteem, at least in theory. I've wondered whether respect for the authority of older family members in my own culture stems from West Africans' view that our elders are the closest to the wisdom of the ancestors. In any case, Life Writers from all backgrounds try instinctually to avoid speaking poorly about their mother, and rightfully so.

So, let's take the time to clarify that this exercise simply allows the younger-you to express herself or himself in ways she or he could not at the time for a variety of reasons. You couldn't afford to look at the disappointing elements in your mother-story then, because at an evolutionary level you knew you relied on her for survival. As this is private writing to yourself, there is no reason not to allow the younger-you to look at this and to speak of it now. I'll go ahead and say that you will very likely develop a whole new perspective of your mother once you work through the feelings generated by your interactions with her, but more on this after the Life Writing process is over.

Also, it is far easier to focus on her perceived shortcomings than it is to re-experience a painful memory the way I'm inviting you to do. It will take some effort to grasp and to do what is asked here. I will continue to guide you.

The reason we go through life without looking back at the experiences I am asking you to revisit, is that as we approach them, we sense their potential power to overwhelm us again. Although there is nothing to be afraid of *now* – it still *feels* that way. We still remember our *stuff* with a child's heart and mind. Part of us remains that child until we get our narrative work done. The narrative work integrates the disappointed child waiting inside and the self you are now.

You have already survived the event that underlies any difficult memory you need to work through, and the very real strength you will gain justifies the decision to revisit the memory of it. Whatever the memory recalls is not real anymore, just remembered. You can feel it, express it, and survive grieving it, however uncomfortable it makes you. You can make the journey to that memory, work through it, and come out stronger on the other side. The process of doing so turns out never to be what was feared. One woman said to me, "I'm afraid I'll start crying and never stop." Rather than an abyss to fall into, however, you will find the floor rises to meet you. Every step toward what is feared counteracts the downward pull and contributes to the ascending process. There is a simultaneous displacement – the pain ends the pain. But you have to take the risk, and go to that difficult memory.

Out of respect for the person you were then in whatever circumstances, some level of mourning is usually necessary in this work. To quote Robin Sharma again, "Change is hard at first, messy in the middle, and gorgeous at the end."

There are no perfect parents. Hear out the little girl or boy inside you. Allow her or him to mourn the truth that she was born perhaps to a woman who never made her feel known and loved. It's very difficult to acknowledge a perception such as "my own mother doesn't love me." The mother's <u>actual</u> feelings are not relevant here; we don't have access to those. The child's perception is what we are after. As Alice Miller put it, "Not to have felt loved just as you truly are cannot heal without mourning." Your mother may not have provided the mothering you were entitled to. You must be able to face this, accept it, and mourn this important loss. Only by grieving it can you stop blaming yourself for it. There is nothing wrong with you. Would the younger you say, "I am sad." or "I am afraid." Or "I am disappointed." Or "I feel rejected." Let her or let him tell you.

This will be hard work for you, but if you do it, you will be left permanently calmer and more peaceful. As you write her or his words, allow yourself to temporarily lose control if you need to—so you can grow strong. Let events happen again in the safety of your grown-up self. Put your finger on just what impacted you and how it impacted you. How did it make you feel? The right word, the one that captures fully and precisely what you felt will pierce your soul and release long-held grief. You can move safely through these memories and finally put them to rest.

No one captures the restorative power of mourning better than Alice Miller who posed these questions in *Drama of the Gifted Child*:

Why does mother go out every evening?

Why does she not take pleasure in me?

What is wrong with me that she prefers to go to other people?

What can I do to make her stay home?

The child you were can cry bitterly now over his loss. Mourning is an important mechanism for change in this work. Remember, you can stop the Life Writing process at any time.

If you do this thoroughly, you will not have to relive your pain again and again - just one good time. You just have to be willing to face it and feel it now that we know what to do with it. Go toward your pain and keep your eyes wide open. Our culture offers you every imaginable way to remain forever out of touch with yourself. Get those words onto the page. Grit your teeth if you have to but write it. Write the dreaded, suspected truth.

TODAY'S WRITING ASSIGNMENT

Today's writing assignment is to first answer the list of questions, then select an episode that epitomizes the most difficult dynamic between you and your mother and show it on the page. This is your private writing.

Here are the questions:

If you do not know the answer to some or all of the questions, what it is like to not know? You may answer this list of questions for other significant mother-figures in your life, but do not omit writing about an absent biological mother.

What three words best describe the woman who became your mother? Select three words that capture her enduring personality.

What were some of her dreams?

What did she want to do with her life? Your best guess, if unknown.

Did she get to meet some of her dreams?

What did she do when she was at home?

Who was she to you when you were a child?

Was she a hugger? If so, what was that like for you? If not, what was that like for you?

What did you want from her that you did not get?

Did she seem to understand you or have a sense of what you needed or wanted? Did she get you?

Were you made to feel special?

Was there ever any question whether she would leave you?

Did she leave? If so, what was that like for you?

Answer the questions, then select an experience that epitomizes the most difficult dynamic between you and your mother and show it on the page.

MY MOTHER STORY

In terms of direct identifiable trauma, the stuff I needed to work through the most was with my dad. I have speculated many times about the impact my mother's pervasive absence, due to her mental illness, had on me. As far back as I can remember, she has always hidden from me when I tried to look into her eyes. She couldn't seem to hold a gaze.

What could that have meant to me when I was an infant? I didn't really learn to relax into and enjoy a gaze myself, until I had grandchildren. I wrote the following poetic piece in honor of this intergenerational loss in my family.

If you've ever seen an infant's interest in your face,

you know she's searching for someone

she expects to find.

One gets the sense that a promise was made.

While the autonomic system attends to the physical body, the infant attunes to the being behind the face she sees.

And when s/he senses that tether between her little heart and yours,

watch him struggle to leap from his own body to you.

Mouth your face in her attempt to get beyond the skin to that bliss she recognizes.

You will never see a more unadulterated ecstasy.

The delightful squeals are a celebration of having been seen here.

That birth was, indeed, merely a bridge on both sides of which she can reside.

Our exit from this life is filled with mystery, and we expect a safe landing somewhere.

So do infants on entry.

She knows that human being is on the inside – a felt experience.

On arrival, she expects to be retained in being,

rather than ejected to some void filled with bodies she cannot enter.

Her seeking it is automated and immediate,

for growth in being is why she was summoned here.

Summoned to a body designed to displace itself

with each passing year with higher qualities of being -

until the body disappears,

leaving the boundaries of human being extended once more.

Finding home inside another – this first accomplishment –

relaxes all creation, for it whispers….

"safe landing".

Up until I did my own narrative work, I would often wake in the middle of the night half way across the floor whimpering, "I want my Mommie." Well, it's your turn now. Thank you for doing your narrative work around your mother experience, and I look forward to continuing the Life Writing process with you in chapter six.

You and Your Mother:

_____

_____

_____

_____

_____

_____

_____

_____

_____

_____

_____

_____

_____

_____

_____

_____

_____

Chapter Six

You and Your Father

The title of this writing session is 'You and your father, with the emphasis on you and not on your father. I will repeat much of what you read in chapter five because it is worth repeating, but also in case you chose to write through your father story first. In this session you will write through some of your experiences with your father, focusing on your most intimate interpretations of those experiences and how they made you feel. The idea is not to imagine or assume that you have understood your father's intentions. The idea is simply to learn and clarify what the younger-you was feeling and thinking. It is important to retain this focus and not fall into delineating what you perceive as his shortcomings.

So, let's take the time to clarify that this exercise simply allows the younger-you to express herself or himself in ways she or he could not at the time for a variety of reasons. You couldn't afford to look at the disappointing elements in your story then, because at an evolutionary level you knew you relied on your father for survival. As this is private writing to yourself, there is no reason not to allow the younger you to look at this and to speak of it now. I'll go ahead and say that you will very likely develop a whole new perspective of your father once you work through the feelings generated by your interactions with him.

Also, it is far easier to focus on his perceived shortcomings than it is to revisit a painful memory the way I'm inviting you to do. It will take some effort to grasp and to do what is asked here. The reason we go through life without looking back at the experiences I am asking you to revisit, is that as we approach them, we sense their potential power to overwhelm us again. Although there is nothing to be afraid of *now* – it still *feels* that way. We still remember our *stuff* with a child's heart and mind. Part of us remains that child until we get our narrative work done. The narrative work, integrates the disappointed child waiting inside and the self you are now.

You have already survived the event that underlies any difficult memory you need to work through, and the very real strength you will gain justifies the decision to revisit the memory again. Whatever the memory recalls is not real anymore, just remembered. You can feel it, express it, and survive grieving it, however uncomfortable it makes you. You can make the journey to that memory, work through it, and come out stronger on the other side. The process of doing so turns out never to be what was feared. One woman said to me, "I'm afraid I'll start crying and never stop." Rather than an abyss to fall into, however, you will find the floor rises to meet you. Every step toward what is feared counteracts the downward pull and contributes to the ascending process. There is a simultaneous displacement – the pain ends the pain. But you have to take the risk, and go to that difficult memory.

Out of respect for the person you were then in whatever circumstances, some level of mourning is usually necessary in this work. To quote Robin Sharma again, "Change is hard at first, messy in the middle, and gorgeous at the end."

There are no perfect parents. Hear out the little girl or boy inside you. Allow her or him to mourn the truth that she was born perhaps to a man who never made her feel known and loved. It's very difficult to acknowledge a perception such as "my own father doesn't love me." The father's *actual* feelings are not relevant here, we don't have access to those. The child's perception is what we are after. To quote Alice Miller, "Not to have felt loved just as you truly are cannot heal without mourning." Your father may not have provided the fathering you were entitled to. You must be able to face this, accept it, and mourn this important loss. Only by grieving it can you stop blaming yourself for it. There is nothing wrong with you. Would the younger you say, "I am sad." or "I am afraid." or "I am disappointed." or "I feel rejected." Let her or let him tell you.

This will be hard work for you, but if you do it, you will be left permanently calmer and more peaceful. As you write her or his words, allow yourself to temporarily lose control if you need to—so you can grow strong. Let events happen again in the safety of your grown-up self. Put your finger on just what impacted you and how it impacted you. How did it make you feel? The right word, the one that captures fully and precisely what you felt will pierce your soul and release long-held grief. You can move safely through these memories and finally put them to rest. Remember, you can stop the Life Writing process at any time.

If you do this thoroughly, you will not have to relive your pain again and again - just one good time. You just have to be willing to face it and feel it now that we know what to do with it. Go toward your pain and keep your eyes wide open. Our culture offers you every imaginable way to remain forever out of touch with yourself. Get those words onto the page. Grit your teeth if you have to but write it. Write the dreaded, suspected truth.

TODAY'S WRITING ASSIGNMENT

Today's writing assignment is to first answer the list of questions, then select an episode that epitomizes the most difficult dynamic between you and your father and show it on the page. This is your private writing.

Here are the questions:

If you do not know the answer to some or all of the questions, what it is like to not know? You may answer this list of questions for other significant father-figures in your life, but do not omit writing about an absent biological father.

What three words best describe the man who became your father? Select three words that capture his enduring personality.

What were some of his dreams?

What did he want to do with his life? Your best guess, if unknown.

Did he get to meet some of his dreams?

What did he do when he was at home?

Who was he to you when you were a child?

Was he a hugger? If so, what was that like for you? If not, what was that like for you?

What did you want from him that you did not get?

Did he seem to understand you or have a sense of what you needed or wanted? Did he get you?

Were you made to feel special?

Was there ever any question whether he would leave you?

Did he leave? If so, what was that like for you?

Answer the questions, then select an experience that epitomizes the most difficult dynamic between you and your father and show it on the page.

MY FATHER STORY

One summer night, my father returned home unusually early and discovered I was out of the house. I was well aware of the strict curfew rules he set for us, although I skirted them as often as I could. The next morning, when he inquired of my whereabouts the night before, I was horror stricken, for a beating in our house was no small business. As usual, he went into one of his beat-out-bad-behavior rages. I muttered something about going to pee and bolted for the front door. I ran crying toward the paper mill across the street. The entire household rushed toward the door. Somehow we all knew I would not be back. My mother whimpered, "Come back, Aihi!" as I heard my dad respond, "Let her go." I looked back, searching to see if his face matched his words. It did, and my heart sank deep into the ground. I climbed into a red trailer and imagined my father trapping me there.

After what seemed like hours, I heard one of my brothers crossing the field nearby and got his attention. I told him I was leaving. Somehow, my younger sisters and brothers and I put me on a bus by nightfall to an older sister's in Los Angeles. I was fifteen. Daddy stopped the beatings after that.

Once when I was three or four years old, I leaned a straight-backed wooden chair against a hedge bush, and climbed into it to sit and read the way my father did when he read the evening paper. Somehow the chair fell backward into the bush, and a branch of the bush pierced through the back of my knee. My father carried me and gently placed me in the back seat of the car before driving me to the hospital. Another time, I was awakened in the middle of the night by a nightmare. In a moment, I was crying and tugging at my parents' covers. My father was startled from his sleep, and in a split-second, lifted me into his arms, held me tightly, then put me down again and said sternly, "Go back to bed." I lay awake the rest of the night remembering the feel of his fast-beating heart against my chest. There must have been other times when I was held by my daddy, but I can't remember them.

It's your turn now. Thank you for doing your narrative work around your father experience, and I look forward to continuing the Life Writing process with you in chapter seven.

<u>You and Your Father:</u>

_____

_____

_____

_____

_____

_____

_____

_____

_____

_____

_____

_____

_____

_____

_____

_____

_____

_____

_____

_____

_____

_____

_____

_____

_____

_____

_____

_____

_____

_____

_____

_____

_____

_____

_____

Chapter Seven

Significant Events

I n this session, you will inventory your past significant traumatic experiences and begin the process of working through them. By now, you are no doubt getting the hang of Life Writing and will be able to use it again and again as a tool for managing the difficult events of your life. We all have them. I Life Write whenever I need to; and it is highly effective in helping me to retain my equilibrium.

Just to bring closure to the last two writing sessions, I want to say that parents don't wake up with the intention to make hell for their children. Their shortcomings are by-products of their own pain and disappointment. It is safe to say that beneath their own hurt, all parents love their children.

Significant events are those events you know you will never forget. They are the life-shaping events of your life. I can't possibly know how to find these events in your life, but you do. This is your opportunity to write about unresolved experiences that I would not know to ask about. What are the difficult events of your life that you know you will never forget? What negative events changed you forever? Which negative experiences still live on in your memory, feeding your understanding of yourself and of the world? Have you had difficult racial experiences? What has taken you the most strength to survive? What secrets do you fiercely protect for fear that others would shun you if they knew? These are just questions to trigger your thinking.

TODAY'S WRITING ASSIGNMENT

What I'd like you to do is to draw a line down the middle of a page. On the left side, list every significant negative episode that you can recall. Just one sentence for each. The ones that were most impactful for you are usually remembered most clearly. On the right side of the page, next to each sentence you wrote on the left side, note the precise emotion you are experiencing in your body as you read that sentence. Identify precisely what you are feeling: Is it fear, shame, rejection, anger, disappointment, embarrassment, disgust, loneliness, betrayal, intimidation, humiliation, dread, anxiety, what is it precisely that you are feeling? The meaning of an event is found by identifying the *precise* emotion that accompanies it.

Now, for today, choose the most difficult one and write about it. Take a deep breath, and begin. What happened? What did it tell you about your worth and value to those involved? How did it make you *feel*? Unwanted? Invisible? Used? Unvalued?

Give yourself time to experience your feelings. Then write them out – onto the page and out of your body and soul.

MY MOST SIGNIGICANT TRAUMATIC EXPERIENCES

The most difficult thing to ever happen to me was hearing my dad say, "Let her go." The second most difficult thing to happen to me was being rejected by an uncle after I was raped. The rape was only the third most difficult thing to happen to me. About a week after it happened, one of my uncles asked me if what he had heard was true. I was naïve enough to think he had heard my version of the event and whispered, "yes." If he had said, "I'm sorry" or hugged me, I think I would have believed I meant something to someone, but he said nothing and rarely spoke to me after that. I was so confused. I wondered why I was so naïve. Why no one told me anything. Why I had to learn such important things by trial and error.

My uncle was like a brother to me. My mother's first children and my grandmother's last children were born around the same time, so he really was like a brother to me. He held that same look in his eyes for me as my uncle Rob, and I loved him so much. Even after I realized that he must have heard a version of the event that was very different than mine, I still couldn't understand how easily he could disconnect from me. As I write these words for you, I realize for the first time the theme of dismissal that runs through both my father story and this one. The wound is opened anew right now, and that is a good thing as I shed these tears. I can immediately link this theme of dismissal to subsequent personal experiences. I consider this to be one of the major losses of my life.

Now, it's your turn. Thank you for doing your narrative work around your traumatic experiences. We are almost done. I look forward to continuing the Life Writing process with you in chapter eight.

<u>Significant Events:</u>

_____

_____

_____

_____

_____

_____

_____

_____

_____

_____

_____

_____

_____

_____

_____

_____

_____

_____

Chapter Eight

Return and Just Write

Chapter eight is called Return and Just Write. Now, you might wonder why I made a whole separate chapter for the instructions I'm about to give you. Well, hopefully, it has been about a week since you completed writing session seven, and you have processed and sufficiently mourned the traumatic experience you wrote about in that session. The processing, mourning, and recovery time for these middle sessions is important, and I didn't want to distract you by the work of writing session eight before you were done with writing session seven.

Today, is a time to go back to sessions four, five, six, or seven and continue to write on any of those topics. Past life-writers requested this time and have found it very useful for continuing the unpacking of previous experiences. You could select the next most traumatic experience from your list and write on that. In any case, most people seem to easily fill the two hours allotted for today's writing assignment.

This assignment wraps up the difficult part of Life Writing. Congratulations for your hard work so far, and thank you for continuing your narrative work to this point. I am very grateful to you and very proud of you. I look forward to switching gears in chapter nine.

Return and Just Write:

_____

_____

_____

_____

_____

_____

_____

_____

_____

_____

_____

_____

_____

_____

_____

_____

_____

Chapter Nine

This, I AM

Y ou have completed the difficult of part of Life Writing. I congratulate you on the real work you have done on your narrative, and I invite you to continue working through your story as new memories rise to consciousness. Pay attention to your dreams as now that the pot is stirred, they can offer unparalleled insights.

Eight writing sessions are not nearly enough to cover everything that is important in your life story, but I have made sure to focus on the critical areas of life experience – areas that are critical for everyone. If you have followed the instructions and allowed yourself to feel deeply and write honestly through your story, you should already feel lighter, more relaxed, and more present, for part of the benefit of Life Writing is immediate. There is also a sleeper effect in the sense that after a few weeks further benefits of Life Writing should emerge. The following questions are meant to help guide you toward these emerging benefits.

Writing Session Nine is titled 'This, I AM'. This session is intended to set you in the direction of some main function in the life you are living. It assumes that there is some unique intention inside your consciousness that will imbue your life with meaning and joy, should you bring it forth in service to humanity, but will leave you with a certain sadness and dissatisfaction with your life if you don't. It assumes that there is a central tendency toward which you gravitate, a strange attractor that calls to you however faint it may be right now. It assumes that there is a theme to your life, an unfolding that can be traced back to the start of your life and back even for generations. This session is designed to help put you in touch with this.

The following questions are meant to be considered patiently. They aren't so much to be answered as contemplated, lived with, carried around in your consciousness as you locate the pieces of a puzzle that is yours alone.

TODAY'S WRITING ASSIGNMENT

The first question is: What "story-in-progress" did you enter at birth, and in what ways are you now trying to make that story better?

THE STORY I ENTERED AT BIRTH

Although he put on a good face for the world and a chuckle in every conversation he had outside our house, my dad was lost in sorrow over the loss of both of his parents, one who he barely met and one who abandoned him at birth. His mother returned to live in our hometown when she was old. I don't think I ever saw her before that, although one particular photo remains in my memory. During a visit home, I drove my dad to her house. My dad grew quieter as we neared. I got the strange sensation of him shrinking there next to me in the seat – my big, tall daddy who always owned the space around him. When I parked the car, I had to coax him out. On the porch, I had to encourage him across the threshold and through the front door. My heart sank as I watched him there, head bowed, silent, scared, longing like a little boy for his mother. He muttered "How ye doin'?" She grunted, "hmph." With lowered eyes and short quick nods, he stole around the edge of the room to safety in the back as I stood helplessly watching. It's why he could let me go. I want all fathers, and all mothers too, of course, to do their narrative work, so no other child has to suffer such words and the look on his face as he said them.

In terms of my mother, I'm convinced that my tendency to look inward stems from my lifelong need to find a way inside her awareness. I'm not quite sure whether she is aware of me the way I hoped, but I did find her to be gentle and creative and deeply intrigued by just about everything. Because of this, I could never quite see any person as just a body, but someone interesting inside to get to know. I can always see so much in a person and am always surprised when a person can't see in themselves at least what I can. My work is about going inward to uncover the beautiful in us for reasons that serve us all. *So what story-in-progress were you born into? In what ways are you now trying to make that story better?*

Next, I want you to *select two experiences in which you experienced flow.* To experience flow is to be in the zone. This is a time when you were so deeply absorbed by what you were doing that you lost all track of time, and rather than being fatigued by it, you were left feeling invigorated and more alive. Select two experiences like this and show them in the manner you have learned to do in Life Writing. Show these experiences rather than tell them. These can be leisure activities, work activities, volunteer activities, art activities, anything. Where were you? What were you doing? How did it feel? Show it.

MY EXPERIENCES OF FLOW

The first experience I would select would be the time I did Life Writing in my best friend's parents' basement. The second would be when I was writing a particular lyrical essay. That was also a Life Writing task in that I was working through raising my daughter alone and her transition to young adulthood. Every time I do anything with Life Writing, I'm in the zone. These aren't stories, I know, but yours should be.

Finally, please identify at least one person, but preferably two people who are living the life you imagine living. For each one, what does he or she do that you wish you could do? For each one, how would you do what this person does differently than the way this person does it?

MODELING MY LIFE

The model for my life is Mirra Alfassa, also known as The Mother. She was Sri Aurobindo's partner. Sri Aurobindo was an Indian guru dedicated to human progress and spiritual evolution. The Mother was also dedicated to spiritual evolution, and she ran the Ashram that Sri Aurobindo founded. I will never reach the stature of The Mother, but she is my model, and I do dream of living in generative community with others. One difference between her vision and mine is something along the lines of spiritual community versus generative community. If I can capture this adequately, I would say hers was a focus on spiritual development for spiritual development's sake whereas my vision focuses on spiritual development for the sake of living well together in community, although these two most certainly overlap.

So who are your role models? They don't have to be famous or anything, just living the life you want to live. Don't select someone based on a single aspect such as strength or courage, but select two people who are living the life you imagine building for yourself.

Once you have a) gained some insight into a particular problem stemming from your early family experience that you might seek to fix, either consciously or subconsciously; b) written out two experiences in which you found yourself in the zone; and c) identified two persons who are living the life you would live if you could, look to see if there is some thread running through all these that connects them somehow. Is there some theme apparent?

It may be that you yourself are just too embedded in your story and experience to achieve such a perspective. You are likely to find some interesting links, though. It might be helpful to select a thoughtful and insightful other person to do this with you - to get someone else to read what you wrote and tell you what emergent themes they see. So, happy writing. In the next and final chapter, we will conclude the Life Writing process.

<u>This, I AM:</u>

_____

_____

_____

_____

_____

_____

_____

_____

_____

_____

_____

_____

_____

_____

_____

_____

_____

Chapter Ten

Conclusion

Well here we are. Forgive me for saying, again, how proud and grateful I am that you have completed this process. If you've done the work, I know we share a knowing that those who have not done their narrative work could never grasp. Because of this, I carry a deep sense of community with all Life Writers. As a Life Writer, you can better help to create the new world in all the ways you touch it – in your family, your relationships, your work, the chance person you encounter in the park. Following Life Writing, your capacity to look kindness into the world must naturally grow and grow, for you have crossed that pivotal threshold from deficiency to being that we discussed in the first session. What kind of world might we create if we were to see it through eyes of non-judgment, of understanding and forgiveness, of unity and communion, joy, and love? What power we have to look all these into places where these are sorely needed.

Life Writing has two parts. You have completed the most important part, but the second part – although it is completely optional - is also very important. In this first part, you have gone inward to yourself – to the younger-you, and allowed him or her to show you her or his long-held pain and to mourn the losses. This first part has loosened the grip those negative memories retained on your continuing growth and development. This first part helps to unblock the energy and information flow through your body, mind, and spirit. It reconnects all the parts of yourself and returns you to your naturally generative evolutionary process.

The *second* part is the voluntary opening of your private story to just one other person who can hear it and weep with you as you show your suffering. Just one person who can feel with you and affirm for you that these difficult experiences do not and cannot speak to what you are worth. This shared recognition of your wrongful loss binds you to the soul of another human being, and can be a potent touch to the psyche that removes the feeling of being fundamentally - alone.

While the first part reconnects the parts of the self, the second part reconnects you to the rest of us. This entire life system is one gigantic organic thing, and the energy and information flowing through you connects in meaningful ways to the energy and information flowing through me and the person next to you, and so on. In the second part of Life Writing, you are invited to allow at least one other person into your private pain - to look with you on what has been mistakenly understood as evidence that you are unworthy – a person who can look right past all this to the real you. Select this person carefully.

MY SOMEONE

My best friend's mother was and is another mother to me. She embraced me from the very beginning as if I was one of her own, and I will forever love her for that. When I finally emerged for good from her basement, I held in my hands the document I'd been writing. Some huge part of the task was finished and everything in me knew that. My truth was on these pages. This was a truth known by no one but me. I wondered whether Momma Leslie would view me differently if she knew all this ugly stuff. I always knew how to make myself look good on the outside. I knew how to make myself look "urban and middle-class" in my efforts to shed the image of a lower-class girl from a small western town. I admired my best friend's family in so many ways. Among other highly admirable qualities, they seemed to epitomize that middle-class ideal so many of us hold. I had to know what would happen if she knew the real me, so I handed her my narrative and told her that this is what I had been doing in the basement all that time. I felt vulnerable for sure. She read it at rapt attention then said, "Aihi, you're such a good writer!" I am still very deeply moved when I recall her open, nonjudgmental, and generous response toward me.

There must be someone like this for you. This person plays an important role in making you feel deeply connected to the human family. If you know someone, have him or her hear or read sessions four, five, six, and seven, and nine (although session nine helps you to detect a theme running through your life story). Let him or her be present with you in your narrative nakedness.

If you don't know someone, look us up at aihisalons.com where we are teaching people how to hear each other's stories, among other things.

A couple more things, then we are done. I want to leave you with one more tool that is guaranteed to support your movement forward from here. In the spirit of Life Writing, I will convey this by way of a story.

I believe my daughter was around eight years old when I started to meditate. I was an avid journaler before that. Journaling showed me the meaning in my experiences and kept me centered. I couldn't re-read the pages. To do so felt like re-living confusion I had so painstakingly clarified, so I never re-read them. They were not for public consumption, not for my grandchildren to read to learn who I am. Journaling was my way of making sense of the day-to-day occurrences in my life, of identifying and understanding my emotions, of remaining at the center of my unfolding story.

The transition from journaling to meditation was seamless. I can't recall what fostered it, but it was my own brand culled together from many readings on the subject and from habits formed during the journaling years. The "journaling" still occurred only I was no longer writing thoughts down. Instead of writing my thoughts of recent occurrences, I watched them. As I did so, whatever was significant, actionable, forgivable, questionable, or the like always emerged. When the thoughts were all gone, not only was I left with the insights I always gained from journaling, but I was also left suspended in this true and splendid silence. That was meditation breakthrough number one – learning the efficiency of meditation over journaling (in my case) and its gift of daily respite.

My intention during the first few years of meditation was to reach the stillness and to remain there for as long as I could afford to on any given day. The most time I ever stayed in one sitting was about three hours, which was glorious. Day after day, through my closed eyes, I reached out to the stillness. Then the second breakthrough occurred. Somehow, rather than reaching out to the stillness, I fell inward and deeply downward into it which took less effort it seemed. The falling deeper and deeper inward felt more natural. For several years now, I have simply fallen farther and farther inward, then the latest breakthrough occurred on February 13th, 2015.

There I was, getting into my morning routine, when it dawned on me that both the far away stillness and the deep down stillness are the same stillness. I thought that perhaps the purpose of meditation is to provide repeated experiences of stillness until we can embody it as we live and interact with each other – until we can actually *be* present as so many spiritual teachers encourage. My hands covered my mouth in surprise. Rather than look for the stillness out there in the universe or deep down inside, I am simply to be the stillness. I wonder whether you grasp this as I wish to convey it? From here, my practice is to be the stillness moment to moment as I live. To be the eternal calm in the midst of living. To rest organically at the center of the stillness as the story unfolds.

In closing, thank you so much, again, for spending this important time with me. I hope to connect with you again.

Love, Aihi.

Overflow Space:

_____

_____

_____

_____

_____

_____

_____

_____

_____

_____

_____

_____

_____

_____

_____

_____

_____

Printed in the United States
By Bookmasters